Brooklyn Astronaut

Inspirational Poems For Kids

WRITTEN BY JERMAIN O. SMITH

EDITED & Illustrated BY TANEICHA S. THOMAS

Brooklyn Astronaut Inspirational Poems For Kids Copyright 2024.
Library of Congress.

All rights reserved to CEO Jermain Smith of Smith Prudent Reads Publishing Company.

No artwork, writing, or anything produced in this project, Brooklyn Astronaut Inspirational Poems For Kids, may be copied, recorded, or massively produced without the owner's consent, in physical writing by a letter. Registered with the Library of Congress.

ISBN's: 979-8-9853866-1-5 (hardcover) | 979-8-9853866-2-2 (paperback) | 979-8-9853866-3-9 (ebook) | 979-8-9853866-4-6 (audio)

Publisher's Cataloging-in-Publication Data

Names: Smith, Jermain O., author
Title: Brooklyn Astronaut : Inspirational Poems for Kids / Jermain O. Smith.
Series: Brooklyn Astronaut Dream Big
Description: Brooklyn, NY: Smith Prudent Reads Publishing, 2024. | Summary: Inspirational poetry about astronauts, the moon, and imagination.
Identifiers: ISBN: 979-8-9853866-1-5 (hardcover) | 979-8-9853866-2-2 (paperback) | 979-8-9853866-3-9 (ebook) | 979-8-9853866-4-6 (audio)

Subjects: Children dreaming| Moon--Juvenile poetry. | Astronauts--Juvenile poetry. | New York (State)--New York—Brooklyn--Juvenile poetry. | Bedford-Stuyvesant (New York, N.Y.)--Juvenile poetry. | Children's poetry. | JUVENILE FICTION / Poetry

Classification: LCC PZ7.S65143 Br 2024 | DDC 811.6--dc23

Publish by Smith Prudent Reads Publishing,
Brooklyn, New York

YOU'RE OUT OF THIS WORLD!

Table of Contents

Dedication 1

Message from the Heart 2

When the Earth Was Alone 4

Dream Big 8

Live the Dream 12

You Can Do It 16

Never Give Up 22

The Magic of Believing 32

Keep Climbing 37

- Almost There 40
- No Limit's 43
- New Beginnings 47
- Don't Forget To Plan 51
- Don't Forget To Pray 54
- Don't Forget To Study Hard 58
- The Beauty Of Your Imagination 63
- Soar High 68
- Student 75

Dedication

I Dedicate this children's book to young teens and adults alike who are pursuing their dreams. Your life experiences will help develop strong work ethic to be an artist or an astronaut. Be honest with Yourself, be vilagaiant, and don't forget to take God with you.

I also want To dedicate this children's book to my personal Lord and Savior Jesus Christ. For without him this project would not have been possible.

I wrote and completed this book of Brooklyn Astronaut INSPIRATIONAL POEMS FOR KIDS and adults alike during a very difficult time in my life. And the Lord has not only sustained me, but let me see my gifts become a light through my words and rhythm to inspire you to plan for your greatness, work hard, pray hard, persevere harder, stay consistent, dedicated, and invest in yourself.

Failure is nothing more then the field of gold mines, full of lessons we stopped digging for. - Jermain O. Smith

A Message From The Heart

In this inspirational series of poetry for kids & young adults alike, we want to encourage you through reading. We hope it lifts your spirits and clears your mind of wasted space.

Promoting positive lifestyle and sparking curiosity. Creative gems in your heart and mind. Put your space boots on, and only stop for new levels of success and watch the STARS!!

Stay focused to be grounded, organized, and sturdy with diet and exercise. Train like the champions and FLY like the Eagles!

A Message From The Heart

I hope you find these poems enjoyable, refreshing and helpful.

May your troubles find its end and you take new flights
to pivot to new adventures and find new loves on your journey.

Above all else, love yourself first 100%,
and have some fun!!

When The Earth Was Alone

When the Earth was alone.
It stood in darkness without the Moon.

When the Earth was alone the lands felt the dry heal from the scorching Sun.

Raging from the Universe imbalanced, this is the collateral damage.

Bruised and burnt lands, abandoned Stars to stand in support of this Earth left all alone.

Inspirational Poems for Girls

Run down habitats, flooding mushy grass, disguised mask amongst trees without leaves.

Hunted down species, wasted food sources, honey spilled over from natural beehives.

When the Earth was Alone, cut off from the Universe, it was reborn as a new Earth in a new Universe.

When The Earth was Alone

With a new Sun & Moon to nurture its core and trillions of stars shining in support of its ne growth.

When the Earth was Alone it healed scorched lands.

It rebuilt damaged property, flooding lands with flourishing wildflowers swaying in its splendor of fields with the bending of the Wind.

Inspirational Poems for Girls

When the Earth was Alone, it formed new mountains, highlands, new foods to support new planets to thrive!

When the Earth Was Alone, it built an unbreakable back bone.

The goodness of Earth's core rebirthed itself deep in the soil that was sown.

When the Earth Was Alone.

Dream Big

Expand and pivot the mind, take it all in, rest and do it again.

This is the magic!

Venture out to explore nicer areas, restaurants, mother nature's beautiful open spaces.

The journey you embark on, is enjoyed when you widen the scope of the Space around you.

Inspirational Poems for Girls

Stay afloat with your thinking never sink the boat.

Aspiring to be the greatest takes time, don't quit on yourself, and you'll become a G.O.A.T.

Don't panic if you trip or slip into the pits, just meditate for a while, you will find an answer that fits.

Collecting new thoughts like oxygen for a new framework to begin.

Dream Big

So Dream Big, expand like the crafted wings of a plane before taking off and soaring to the big beautiful blue sky winds!

Thinking Big strengthens your Fatih & your heart to be fearless.

No push backs, or tight ropes, let your inner child room free like parrots at the sea carefree.

Inspirational Poems for Girls

On another journey of Big Dreams that never ends!

Full of life another purpose has begun, like the birth of flowers in spring that blossom.

Or in a hot air balloon with a silly clown.

Keep creating and adding to your Big Dreams.

Live The Dream

Don't just
Dream Big,
Live the
Dream!

Spoil yourself like your
favorite scoop of ice
cream.

Staying consistent
aligning inner strength
you can rely on and trust.

When having goals with
a definite Why,

Inspirational Poems for Girls

Everyone you love may not come by, so get prepared to say a hard good bye, flap your wings and fly high.

The Dream is real, it's just on a temporarily hold, so have patience as your creativitely grows. Stand nearby so you are ready to go.

Eliminate any fears you're the Giant! The champion, the Big Polar Bear to be revered.

Living The Dream

So stay disciplined, and follow a mentor, a teacher that has proven their authority.

Your mentor is suppose to find your faults don't let it be disheartening.

Pay attention and listen, while your peers parlay in distraction, you will gain real traction!

While others become lily lackers & fight for time wasted for a fraction of what's gone.

Inspirational Poems For Girls

You'll stand tall like a tree in all seasons because you took daily action!

Pretty soon, you'll go from weary thoughts to skipping steps & smiling.

Living the dream in your purpose, dancing, rejoicing and living the rest of your life as a Champion.

Living the Dream.

You Can Do It

God has given you everything you need to succeed.

A brain, hands, eyes, and feet are your precious tangible gifts!

All other gifts and talents are a Bonus.

A can do attitude requires belief in your abilities to work hard at your passion.

Inspirational Poems for Girls

Don't be swayed instead be prudent and read often.

Real champions sometimes bleed going without wants and needs.

Sacrifices to being a warrior requires, praying knees & hands working together.

You were given different tools than the forefathers.

You Can Do It

Persevere, work hard and keep a beautiful heart, mind and spirit.

Use the steam that made you mad as fuel to be of service to others and help make the community strong and upright.

Check in with yourself, in those moments you grow impatient, lonely or sad, don't react stay motivated. Destiny is quickly calling so make haste and catch a cab.

Inspirational Poems for Girls

You can do it you got this, keep working late in your lab.

From the window pane, let the naysayers stare, years from now they will still be there.

Let your work ethic speak for you, like a sword quiet & strong and let your accomplishments show them why you belong.

Stay Demur, Classy with a touch of sweet sassy.

You Can Do It

You can do it, you hold brilliant ideas & dreams, like sweet marshmallows & hot cocoa in a Brooklyn Astronaut mug.

You can do it. Don't shrug your destiny off like an annoying bug.

Start working, researching for your personal styles, Like NAS the rapper,

 Be Illmatic!

Inspirational Poems for Girls

Your breakthrough, will be as beautiful as a pink, orange and white pillow like sky before it turns morning blue. You got what it takes, you can & will do it.

All that's left now is to apply and simply do.

You Can Do it!

Never Give Up

Staying in it for the long haul. This is not a race, but a marathon.

So don't forget to budget your time, breathe slowly and take deep breaths.

Inspirational Poems For Girls

Sweat rolling down your back, legs and hands, as you ponder a path and switch lanes.

Hate from others can't prosper because God Is with you.

Use your divine gifts he placed in your hands, words and your life itself.

Stay in prayer when you need real suppport from the one

Never Give UP 24

who hangs the in world in outer space like a light bulb.

Who has created the mountains and heavens over the seas, surely he is able to love and take care of thee.

Hardships is life doing you a favor, to distinguish your real enemies from your true cheerleaders.

Inspirational Poems For Girls

Keep like minded pioneers around you who are building something special of their own.

Mentors and peers you can actually reach out to and get on the phone.

Don't seek them out, be patient let them present themselves like the Elf on the Shelf.

Never Give UP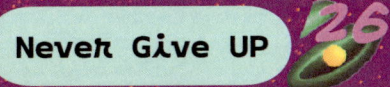

Never Give Up,

Let the Chaos fuel your determination to win.

Through harsh hurricane winds, stand firm and prove them wrong.

Never Give Up!

We all have growing pains and trails at some point.

Just hold on to the rope of faith just a little bit longer.

Inspirational Poems For Girls 27

Wrap your legs one by one, use the loop, and pull up and scoot and pull until you're high as an Owl and yell,
    Hoolie Whooo!

Here I am, currently disabled, depressed, betrayed and thrown away, labeled an outlaw and an outcast just a place to be someone's punching bag.
Some will speak down to you, because their self-esteem is low, they have no plans to to reach their goals.

Never Give UP 28

It makes them feel good if they can distract you from your dreams. Be firm, God is on your team.

You were not born to be a punching bag, filled with scorn, trauma bombs, love bombs and land mines.

You have purpose and power over your life, you're as important as the air you breathe.

Inspirational Poems For Girls

Don't let their darkness enrage or persuade you to miss a step.

Don't change, know that you are royal, and always qualify who can be in your circle. You are the light, that's why they attack you.

This is a battle, they can't take away what God has already put on the inside of you.

Let no one tame, blame or game you out of your passion.

Never Give UP

Be a lighthouse that shines in good and bad weather.

Continue to be real and authentic for you, always bet on you.

Never Give Up

because once you learn how to build it they can never take those skills way from you.

Take time to find your greatness like Shields & Richardson to become world class citizens, that's going to be reality show.

Never Give Up!

Inspirational Poems For Girls

Journal your Dreams, Goals & Aspirations

BROOKLYN ASTRONAUT SIGN UP FOR THE DREAM BIG DIGITAL JOURNAL MEMBERSHIP!!!

Journal your Dreams- Goals, Aspiration

Journal your Dreams- Goals, Aspiration
Journal your Dreams- Goals, Aspiration
Journal your Dreams- Goals, Aspiration
Journal your Dreams- Goals, Aspirations
Journal your Dreams- Goals, Aspirations
Journal your Dreams- Goals, Aspiratio

The Magic Of Believing

The Magic of Believing has my soul in a joyous gleam.

I feel like I'm bouncing from star to star.

As I skip & sing and shine like Bling Bling

From a Prince or Princess and a King or a Queen wearing their crown.

Inspirational Poems For Girls

Not with the get down, serious content with no frown.

But not all the time, your smile is like the rare season where the sun is barely shown, after the rain and clouds are gone.

A leader, a captain of your own land with depth, like the brass sound baritone in a live band.

The Magic of Believing is having confidence in being different.

The Magic of Believing

The path to independence is often met with interference.

Watch where your footsteps lead you. Goons & trouble makers want to block your entrance.

The Magic Of Believing will breakthrough and cut through every dark season.

Cutting down & bagging up all the garbage, rising above painted imagery that you are a savage.

Inspirational Poems For Girls

We live among corrupt people living lavishly temporarily.

Before you know it, they will be locked up for treachery, deceit & selfish ignorance for trying to steal the cream from your dream!

Beware, some of us have sunk into the division among ourselves, from the damage that life sometimes causes.

The Magic of Believing

Don't let outside forces stop the flow, it's tougher if you don't grow.

But guess what, you are just as tough as what you go through! The journey gets difficult, just stay on course.

Weather the winter storms so you can do cartwheels in the Sun. Never stop Believing in you and your Big Dreams!

The Magic of Believing

Keep Climbing

Bruised knees, dirty shoes, frustration sinking in negative attitudes.

Bruised hands, fatigued legs, searching & begging for a better way, an easier or quicker route, parched lips as you sip your water beverage, nearly out.

It looks so far away, how will I make it through the day.

Inspirational Poems For Girls

Grey clouds hid the sun, it's OK to rest, but your never done.

Just one foot in front of the other young hearts, focus on today's travels, so future plans don't come apart.

The journey is the experience lived one day at a time.

So keep Climbing, with consistency you have already won!

Keep Climbing

Post your flag on the top of the mountain, and take in the views because you kept climbing.

You kept giving yourself encouragement daily to strengthen you for the journey. They will never tell you, but you are secretly motivating those around you.

Keep Climbing

Almost There

The pressure is hard here, you can feel it.

Just remember to breathe in the high tension challenging moments.

Almost There, but your arms are barely moving.

Space surfing energy is failing, so get anchored to positive thoughts as you sweat and labor for your passion.

Inspirational Poems For Girls

Your inner child says, Oh stop complaining & pace yourself for the end of the race.

Don't sprint, jog with your earbuds in listening to your favorite song.

Kick off the run with everything within you. Focus & breathe before crossing the finish line to a victorious win.

Almost There 42

Congratulations you saw it through to the end, you are here with the winners and not with the quitters.

Break free of the hate and judgment celebrate and sing out loud and proud!

Almost There, now you are here!
Congratulations again on your win and you can do it over and over again.

Almost There!!

No Limit's

Have potential like sugar unstirred at the bottom of the lemonade jug.

You have great soil for growth, avoid those with no seeds in the ground that listen to negative bugs.

Many will never understand their value , and will move at the pace of a slouch with No .stars to chase.

Inspirational Poems For Girls

To manifest the Gold and treasures you need a shovel of faith to dig until ground breaks.

Until your purpose or mission are discovered, your future is safely locked away like,

Grandma's pumpkin & apple cookies & pies.

No Limit's

No limits, you can be whatever you set your heart & mind to.

Let your Faith manifest your sweet destiny.

No limits, even if it's been done again and again. See, they can't have your fingerprint brand identity.

Be innovative & creative take advantage of social programs. No limits among the stars in outer space.

Inspirational Poems For Girls

Limit your time dwelling in a negative mindset that does not believe, it's just a little fear creeping in.

Get around a pool of winners. A team of masterminds looking for new planets of endless possibilities and arriving on new planets of hope. There truly is no limit, remember your Universe is Yours!

No Limits

The Sky Is The Beginning

Clear blue skies, angelic songs the birds sings.

Peaceful clouds floating like birthday party balloons.

Filling you up with light, your vision is so amazing, funny & entertaining.

Moving in faith will help you maintain your focus.

Inspirational Poems For Girls

Stand still in place of warmth from the gold sun.

It's like seeking the love from a home cooked meals with a second and third helping.

Still emerging in experiences & understanding, while curiosity stirs your learning.

Keep flowing and growing with an intentional force into the wind.

The Sky Is The Beginning

Then you'll see and pivot to new states of maturity, when

So keep reaching, far like as Astronaut from Brooklyn soaring to outer worlds.

Let's keep seeking and evolving into greatness.

Better versions of our old mental programing that's unfruitful & can not serve your new growth.

Inspirational Poems For Girls

The Sky is the beginning, don't you see?

The Sky Is the beginning, there's a whole universe to create & explore.

Becoming more, and more aspiring to dream, living the myths seen in social media, their fantasies will be your reality.
Growing more and more as you reach for the star.

The Sky Is The Beginning

Don't Forget To Plan

Humanity does not know your future, but you have one.

One thing for certain is you will not have one, unless it's' planned.

For the gift of our eyes and ears, to give ourselves over to learning to plan & map out our dreams.!

Locate the Beginning before you start your journey.

Inspirational Poems For Girls

So you can have a smart calculated decision.

A bird's eye view of the chess board, before a piece is even played.

The same way the coach gets the team in practice everyday.

Don't Forget to plan, write down your vision & set goals.

Don't Forget To set long term & short term goals.

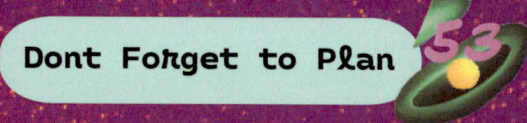

Dont Forget to Plan

This will instill confidence and keep you out of the cold.

Don't Forget to fold your clothes & keep your room neat & organized, your personal environment will set the tone.

A clutter house is like a cluttered mind and unwritten thoughts is a confused closed mind.

Set the pencil to the pad, for clarity before you execute and begin.

Don't Forget to Plan.

Don't Forget To Pray

Ambition like a pure white flame, within the fireplace of my heart of passion, it feels like home.

Seeking higher ground for clarity helps you tap into safe spaces to pray and strengthen your spirits.

Inspirational Poems For Girls

Without God everything would be impossible but, with

God all things are possible & ready to manifest.

Humbly avoid beating your chest, his presence relieves all stress and from the Great I Am Majesty, I receive rest.

When confused & life seems complex, find real guidance & strength in prayer.

Dont Forget To Pray

So hit your knees or fold your arms, sit still and hold tight and pray small prayers to cover your life.

Don't Forget to Pray over your plans, so our Heavenly Father can rain down blessings of increase and favor over your life.

Don't Forget to Pray & give gratitude, thanks for all gifts and talents given to you.

Inspirational Poems for Girls

Don't Forget to Pray for your protection whenever you travel.

Don't Forget to Praise him in moments of trouble, know it's working out for your good in due time.

In All of your goals, achievements and endeavors, Don't Forget to Pray, to your Heavenly Father in which all life and Blessings flows freely through him.

Don't Forget to Pray

Don't Forget To Study Hard

Even if you skip the line to the university, you can't escape the Universal Law that knowledge is necessary.

To ignore the studious section of your gifts, will keep your energy low. Without insight to properly execute plans, the system will lack tools & processing power to grow.

Inspirational Poems For Girls

Hard headed because you refuse to listen, unable to bust a move and quickly you start to lose.

Stay focus, all Is not lost, you can change your perception for a direction.

Be patient, stay the course. Work & study hard. Keep tapping at the brick stony wall. A few more inches, before the tresure falls.

Don't Forget To Study Hard

P, Let your progress gives you peace, to settle the pressure and anxiety.

Dont be surprised when others dont rejoice, stay to yourself and prioritize your activities & goals.

Keep putting one foot in front of the other, take it one day at a time. Failing to leverage time as a resource can cost your precious dimes.

Inspirational Poems For Girls

Take a deep breath, make it a practice to retreat to a relaxed state of mind.

Set order like a gingerbread house, make sure you secure your heart against controversy winds and stand firm.

It's challenging, but just take one step at a time. Free your mind give yourself time to listen & learn how to grind! And pretty soon you'll start to earn as your yearn to become a positive influence to those who come around.

Don't Forget To Study Hard

When the seed becomes a tree, and the fruit is finally ripe, success is like the sweet mango picked fresh in the sunlight.

Congratulations you stayed committed and have seen it through to the end, your work ethic is a true gem.

Refreshing your spirit from your harvest after the rains so you can me strong tomorrow to do it again.

Don't Forget To Study Hard

The Beauty Of Your Imagination

Let's Fly to different galaxies.

Let's explore Life's shifting Realities

Let's go outside of the neighborhood.

Let's go outside the norm, don't be dull, sharpen your wits.

Inspirational Poems For Girls

Let your thoughts sway in the beautiful Tulip flowers.

With all of these pleasurable ideas your mind creates, it can wander far.

Another adventure your imagination embarks upon from alien jelly fish to magical mermaids designed in sparkling glitter scales.

The Beauty Of Your Imagination

A space in the heart of your imagination where creativity inhabits.

Visualize positive images and practice dreaming. Visualize your future consistently.

Until you walk with the light breeze Of your imagination, sitting under a beach umbrella with your toes wiggling in the sand with ease.

Inspirational Poems For Girls

Until the sunrise and sunset become your daily appreciated scenery.

The heaviness of your eyelids start to snooze.

As the calm of the ocean waves like beach seashells into your soul breathes life.

Painting canvases from blank notebook thoughts, leaving it filled with color that emerges & intertwines.

The Beauty Of Your Imagination

The Beauty of Your Imagination, is the beauty of your mind. It's a rare jewels of pearls, locked in a shell resting on a ocean floor.

Unlock the mind & limitless living through the beauty of your mind and its imagination.

Keep your imagination close to your heart never let the world pull it apart.

The Beauty Of Your Imagination

Soar High

Soar High
towards the Ocean
blue sky,

as free as the Eagles flies,
from the east, west, north
& south side.

Soaring High above enemy
lines, build forts to defend
your tribe, legacy & lifeline.

Soar High above the conflict,
get a bird's eye view
perspective.

Inspirational Poems For Kids

Don't wallow with the chickens. Don't get muddy with the piglets, unless you're starting a farm.

Sour High above turbulence, like a Merchant you have confidence, you set the trends like 911 Emergencies..!!

You were born to thrive above dark clouded comments & false roomers and yucky disturbing personalities.

Soar High 70

Thunderstorms that leave you feeling gloomy in your bedroom.

Just stand tall and stay strong, focus on the mission.

Massive action taken to hate, But keep loving on the reality of your success.

In the midst of persecution, a sign of transformation in the autumn season, leaves me to believe in better days.

Inspirational Poems for Girls

For Soaring High, peeling off old reptile skin, hibernating in greatness like a bear in its den.

The level of attack, will revive your value as Eagle, overlooking the valley from your skyscraper mountain nest in a tree planted in the stone.

Keep an appetite for royal excellence you will never be prey. Wipe your mouth clean from the dishes because you just ATE.

Soar High 🛸 72

Gliding & swooping through the sky, established a Legacy as a Queen in own your Galaxy.

Focus on the love & the strength from your CORE it's a one of a kind source of intuition GPS.

Admiration from the beauty of your wings when the sun shines upon you.

Ooh how the reflection of light glistens and dances among your thick colorful feathers,

Inspirational Poems for Girls

Leading the pack of Eagles that follows from the next generation.

Victorious over the concrete Jungle, letting your voice echo in the midst of the mumbo jumbo.

Freeing the misunderstood from the lies of loud forces, with their limiting beliefs always reach out to a healing reef.

Soar High 🏞️ 74

Soaring High, to new levels and new depths.

Soaring High among the clouds & trees.

Soaring High, you were born for this, you waited & prepared your whole life for this.

Soar High like the Eagle effortlessly gliding through the wind, always continuing to thrive to be a champion.

Soar High.

Student

Don't get into a confined index of thinking.

To be a real scholar, The World is YOUR classroom

From the bushel of autumn red, brown & yellow leaves. To the pond where the toad lives.

Inspirational Poems For Girls

76

To the lake where the mountains watch the views.

To the injustice & broke homes. Stolen jewels, by some cruel dudes..

Don't mingle with the wrong things, in the wrong places, at the wrong time you will find monsters with appetites that drools over your food! Don't let them steal your joy.

Student

They don't want duel, so they make issues then look around you.

When you walk among the world, never consistently walk with your head down, keep your crown UP straight not down on devices.

Pay attention look around. Never go the same way twice.

Inspirational Poem for Girls

You can do anything you set your mind to. Just change the questions of self doubts that you listen to.

Like, how will I get it done? Instead, ask who has succeeded and won, and find Mentors in your interest to follow and learn from!

Our history isn't meant to create hate through emotional lenses.

79

Our history is to show our people stories of strength & resilience as a nation and the beauty of what togetherness holds.

Don't let the ugliness of others ruin your beautiful creativity inside you.

Always evolving, maturing, learning and being made whole.

Student

HOPE YOU HAD A GOOD DAY!

SCAN QR CODE TO JOURNAL ABOUT GOOD DAYS, DREAMS & PLANS